AN A-MAZE-ING FARM ADVENTURE

BY JILL KALZ ILLUSTRATED BY MATTIA CERATO

PICTURE WINDOW BOOKS
a capstone imprint

START

FINISH

Designer: Lori Bye
Art Director: Nathan Gassman
Production Specialist: Jane Klenk
The illustrations in this book were created digitally.

Picture Window Books
151 Good Counsel Drive
P.O. Box 669
Mankato, MN 56002-0669
877-845-8392
www.capstonepub.com

Library of Congress Cataloging-in-Publication Data
Kalz, Jill.
   An a-maze-ing farm adventure / by Jill Kalz ; illustrated by
Mattia Cerato.
      p. cm. — (A-maze-ing adventures)
   Includes index.
   ISBN 978-1-4048-6038-4 (library binding)
   1. Farms—Juvenile literature. 2. Domestic animals—Juvenile
literature. 3. Map reading—Juvenile literature. I. Cerato, Mattia,
ill. II. Title.
   S519.K365 2011
   793.73'8—dc22
                              2010019462

Printed in the United States of America in North Mankato, Minnesota.
112010
006017R

WELCOME TO THE
A-MAZE-ING FARM

Here's what you do: Use your finger to make your way through each maze from start to finish. If a person, tree, or other object blocks your way, choose a different path. It's **OK** to use the bridges and ladders. The star in the lower left corner of each maze shows direction. It's called a compass rose. The boxes with tiny pictures are called keys or legends. They'll help you find barns, chicken coops, wagon rides, and more.

What's that silly dog up to? See if you can spot him sneaking through each maze.

Answers start on page 26.

RADAR

On the Farm

Time for chores! First, use the key to find the chicken coop, and collect the eggs. Next, find the grain bins, and gather lunch for the cows. Is the greenhouse west or east of the farmer's house? North or south of the two apple-pickers?

FINISH

KEY

🐓 Barn		🌿 Greenhouse	
🐔 Chicken Coop		🏠 House	
🌾 Grain			

5

Corn Confusion

Keeping the critters out of the corn is a full-time job. Are the three raccoons west or east of the Finish? Which direction is the running deer from the compass rose? Can you spot the three pitchforks?

START

FINISH

7

Ponies in a Pickle

The ponies are puzzled. Can you find your way through these fences? Which building is farthest south? Farthest east? Is the training area north or south of the boy flying a kite?

START

8

KEY

🐓 Barn   ◉ Machine Shed

🏠 House   Ⓤ Training Area

🌾 Grain

FINISH

9

Tulip Tangle

Walk, skip, or tiptoe through the tulips! How many bridges are west of the Start? How many are east? Can you find the four people without a flower basket?

START

10

START

12

Hey, Hey! It's Hay!

Raise the barn roof, and peek inside. Use the key to find the tack room. It holds all the horse-riding gear. Which direction are the cows from the hay loft? Can you spot all six metal pails?

KEY

(⊘) Hay Loft   (⊗) Workshop

(🐴) Tack Room

FINISH

13

START

14

Roundabout Rice

What grows in this soggy field? Rice! Stick to the skinny green path from the Start sign to the Finish sign. And be sure to wave at the 11 water buffalo. Is the compass rose north or south of the biggest hut? Which direction is the dog from that hut?

FINISH

START

16

Lost in Lavender

Ahhh ... this field of purple flowers smells like perfume! Most of the lavender pickers have filled their baskets. But can you spot the 10 empty baskets? Is the man wearing a cap west or east of the woman wearing a bright pink shirt?

FINISH

Ziggy Zaggy Piggies

Can you wiggle around these pigs without wallowing in the mud? Which direction is the boy in the red shirt from the woman in the yellow shirt? Which direction is she from the dog? The Start? The sun?

START

18

START

20

Dairy Farm Detour

Mmm-morning! These dairy cows are ready to be mmm-milked! Which is farther west—the milking parlor or the tanker trucks? If you're standing by the Finish, which direction do you have to go to get to the bulk tanks?

FINISH

KEY

C Computer

🏠 Milking Parlor

📋 Bulk Tank

🕐 Tanker Truck

21

Pumpkin Patch Puzzle

Pose with a scarecrow. Catch the beat of the local band. Share some fall festival food. And whoop it up on a wagon ride. Which direction are the gift shops from the ticket booth? Can you find all nine sunflowers?

BIGGEST

START

22

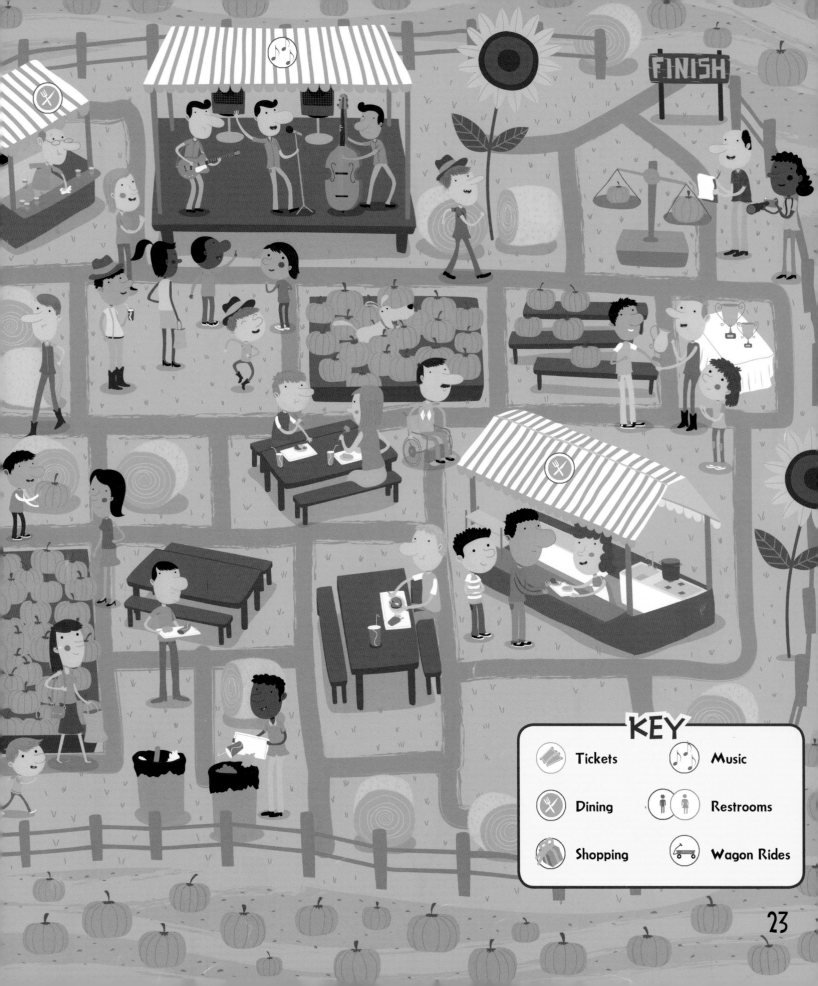

FINISH

KEY

Tickets		Music	
Dining		Restrooms	
Shopping		Wagon Rides	

23

START

24

Baffled by Apple Trees

Apple trees sleep all winter—and they miss all the snowy fun! Is the two-person sleigh west or east of the snowmen? West or east of the compass rose? See if you can find the seven sleds.

FINISH

25

MAZE ANSWERS

On the Farm (page 4-5)

Corn Confusion (page 6-7)

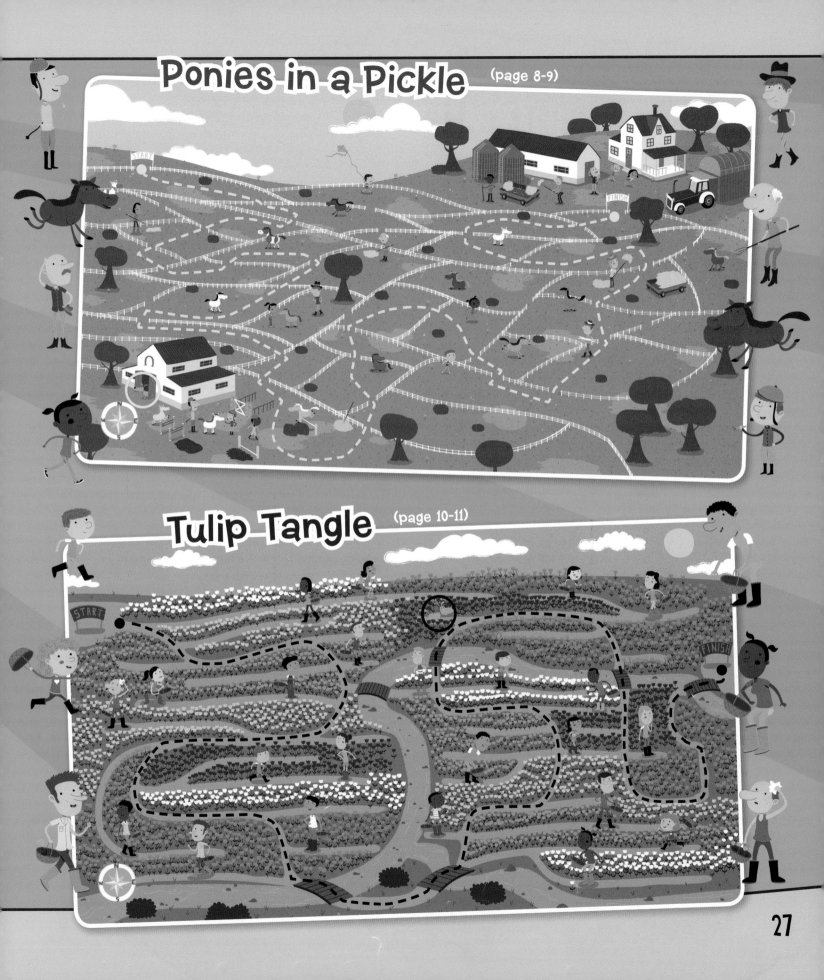

Ponies in a Pickle (page 8-9)

Tulip Tangle (page 10-11)

Hey, Hey! It's Hay! (page 12-13)

Roundabout Rice (page 14-15)

Lost in Lavender (page 16-17)

Ziggy Zaggy Piggies (page 18-19)

MAZE ANSWERS

Dairy Farm Detour
(page 20-21)

Pumpkin Patch Puzzle
(page 22-23)

Baffled by Apple Trees (page 24-25)

TO LEARN MORE

More Books to Read

Blair, Beth L. *The Everything Kids' Gross Mazes Book: Wind Your Way Through Hours of Twisted Turns, Sick Shortcuts, and Disgusting Detours!* An Everything Series Book. Avon, Mass.: Adams Media, 2006.

Heimann, Rolf. *Mega Mazes.* New York: Sterling Pub. Co., 2006.

Munro, Roxie. *The Wild West Trail Ride Maze.* Albany, Tex.: Bright Sky Press, 2006.

Internet Sites

FactHound offers a safe, fun way to find Internet sites related to this book. All of the sites on FactHound have been researched by our staff.

Here's all you do:

Visit *www.facthound.com*

Type in this code: 9781404860384

Look for all the books in the A-MAZE-ing Adventures series: